I0566931

THE VOLUNTEER'S GUIDE TO
KIDMIN

Your Role and
Its Eternal Impact

Corey Jones

KIDZMATTER
PUBLISHING

The Volunteer's Guide to KidMin: Your Role and Its Eternal Impact

Copyright ©2024 by Corey Jones

All Rights Reserved. No portion of this book may be reproduced in any form without written permission from the publisher or author, except as permitted by U.S. copyright law.

Published by KidzMatter
432 East Val Lane, Marion, IN 46952

kidzmatter.com

Printed in the United States of America

Cover Design and Book Layout by Nicole Jones, kneecoalgrace@gmail.com

All scriptures are taken from the Holy Bible, New Living Translation, Copyright © 1996, 2004, 2015 by Tyndale House Foundation. Used by permission of Tyndale House Publishers, Inc., Carol Stream, Illinois 60188. All rights reserved.

Some portions of this book were refined with the assistance of AI technology. While aided by AI tools, this book represents the author's original work and creative expression.

ISBN: 979-8-9850095-9-0

CONTENTS

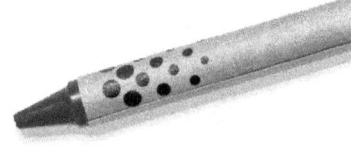

called to make a
DIFFERENCE

You have answered a call — a call to invest in the future, to shape young hearts, to make an eternal impact. As a KidMin volunteer, you hold an incredible influence and responsibility. This guide is dedicated to equipping you with the tools and encouragement needed not simply to participate in children's ministry, but to thrive within it. It's time to redefine what it means to be a KidMin volunteer, moving beyond a childcare mindset to embracing the heart of a minister. Within these pages, you'll discover practical strategies for connecting with kids on a deeper level, preparing engaging lessons, and partnering with parents. This is more than just a job; it's a calling, a mission field ripe for harvest. Let's dive in and discover the profound impact you can make in the lives of children, leaving a legacy that echoes into eternity.

The Why Behind the What

You may be wondering, "Why should I, as a volunteer, invest my time in children's ministry?" It might seem like a small thing in the grand scheme of "adulting," with endless to-do lists and responsibilities. But what if you could be a part of something eternally significant? What if your service, your laughter, your simple act of showing up could make a difference not just for a Sunday morning, but for eternity?

You are in the people business, not the program business. Every interaction, every smile, and every story shared with a child plants a seed. You might not see it bloom overnight, it sometimes takes a generation to see significant results. But your faithfulness, your willingness to be a part of something bigger than yourself has ripple effects reaching far beyond what you can imagine.

The world is hungry for authenticity, for people who are willing to be real, to be present, to simply care. When you invest in a child's life, you are showing them the love of Jesus in tangible ways. You're creating a safe space for them to ask questions, to explore their faith, and to experience the joy of being a part of a caring community.

Don't underestimate the power of your presence, your time, and your love.

"So, my dear brothers and sisters, be strong and immovable. Always work enthusiastically for the Lord, for you know that nothing you do for the Lord is ever useless."
-1 Corinthians 15:58

More Than Babysitters

Many people view children's ministry as a less important role in the church. Sometimes children's ministry is seen as just childcare, while the "real" ministry happens with adults. The truth is discipling children is one of the most important things a church can do. When you pour into the lives of children, you are shaping the church.

There's a common misconception that children's ministry is primarily about crayons, snacks, and entertaining children while their parents attend the main service. While those elements may have their place, they should never over-shadow the heart of children's ministry: making disciples who make disciples.

Children's ministry is about creating an atmosphere where young hearts connect with Jesus on a personal level. It's about nurturing their faith, equipping them to live out their faith in a world that often challenges their beliefs. It's about partnering with parents, and recognizing that parents are the primary spiritual influencers in their children's lives.

This means shifting the focus from simply entertaining children to equipping them to be world-changers who carry the message of Jesus into their schools, homes, and communities.

Eternal Significance

On your list of everything you will accomplish today, what will matter next year? What will make a difference in a decade? How about eternity? Serving the next generation and introducing them to Jesus matters more than you will ever know. You may see a child accept Christ and their eternity change, but there is no way to see all the people that child will impact and the ripples this one decision will make for all eternity.

The vast majority of people will decide to follow Jesus Christ as Lord and Savior between the ages of 4 and 14, positioning children's ministry as a mission field with supreme importance. Even when the results aren't immediately visible, preschoolers are soaking up information... growing in their hearts and heads. They are learning who Jesus is and all about His love for them. Elementary kids are engaging God's story. They are at a stage where they can begin to understand the narratives within the Bible and relate them to their own lives. And preteen students are affirming their identities in Christ, seeking a safe space to process their doubts as they transition from childhood to adolescence.

Instead of viewing children's ministry as simply a stepping stone to adult ministry, shift your mindset. Recognize it as a foundational and pivotal mission field. Understand that each moment spent teaching, comforting, and guiding a child is an investment in their eternal journey, planting seeds of faith that will flourish throughout their lives and into eternity. Your dedication today shapes the spiritual landscape of tomorrow.

"So let's not get tired of doing what is good. At just the right time we will reap a harvest of blessing if we don't give up."
-Galatians 6:9

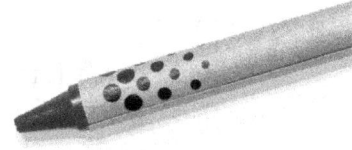

understanding your role
and stepping into
SIGNIFICANCE

Serving in children's ministry is a high calling, not a consolation prize or a box to check. Those who serve in children's ministry are not simply filling a slot, but Purpose Partners, playing a crucial role in shaping the future of the church. Every interaction with a child is an appointment. Children are not an interruption.

Leaders, I want to encourage you to view yourself as passengers in the car of a family's faith journey. We often treat our ministries like school buses, picking kids up, doing our own thing, and then dropping them off without interacting with the parents. Instead, recognize parents are driving the discipleship in their child's life and come along side them. Build intentional strategies to equip and empower parents to lead their children spiritually. Engage parents as partners in discipleship. This doesn't have to be a complicated program or spreadsheet. You can simply start a conversation with a parent about their child and listen to their heart.

Meaningful Connections

One of the most impactful ways to create lasting change in the lives of children is by fostering meaningful and personal connections with them. While large group activities and structured lessons have their place, it's the individual interactions which often leave the most significant mark.

In a large group setting, it's easy for children, especially those who are shy or introverted, to feel lost in the crowd. Individual attention tells a child they are important and worth someone's time.

With a little intentionality, kids feel seen and valued.

Volunteers who engage with children on a more personal level, learning about their interests, struggles, and dreams create a foundation for authentic relationships to develop. When a child feels connected to a caring adult, they are more likely to be open and receptive to the messages being shared.

Practical Tips to Encourage Meaningful Connections

Intentional Conversation: Go beyond surface-level conversations. Instead of just asking "How was your day?," ask more specific questions like "What was the funniest thing that happened today?" or "What's one thing you're looking forward to this week?"

Shared Activities: Engage with children in activities they enjoy, like playing games, reading books, or working on art projects. This shared experience strengthens the bond and creates positive memories.

Presence over Programs: While structured activities are important, prioritize being fully present with children. Put aside distractions, listening attentively, and engaging wholeheartedly in the moment, even if it means deviating from the planned schedule.

Consistency is Key: For relationships to deepen, consistency is crucial. Serve regularly so that children can anticipate and rely on your presence. Yes, it's okay to go on vacation or to care for a sick family member, but on the days where you are simply tired, remember there are little ones who anticipate seeing you and just your presence will minister to them.

By prioritizing meaningful connections, you create a children's ministry where every child feels seen, loved, and empowered to grow in their faith.

Beyond the Surface

Children, like adults, are complex beings who carry a mixture of joys and burdens. It's easy to be captivated by their infectious laughter and playful energy, but we need to see beyond the surface and recognize the hidden anxieties children carry. Looking beyond the surface is crucial for fostering genuine connection and spiritual growth.

Imagine Trey, a lively ten-year-old who loves to participate in games and activities. He's always eager to lend a helping hand and quick to make friends. However, beneath his cheerful demeanor, Trey carries the weight of his parents' recent separation. The familiar routine of his life has been disrupted, leaving him feeling insecure and anxious about the future.

While Trey might not articulate these feelings directly, his subtle changes in behavior provide clues. He might be more withdrawn during small group discussions, easily frustrated during activities, or unusually quiet at pick-up time when his parents arrive separately. These changes, though seemingly small, can signal a deeper struggle requiring attention and care.

You play a vital role in creating a safe and supportive environment for children like Trey. You are the boots on the ground and will be the first to recognize both verbal and nonverbal cues that indicate a child might be struggling. It's important to practice active listening, creating a safe space for children to share their feelings, and responding with empathy rather than judgment.

Serving in kid's ministry is a high calling, full of joy and challenges. Think of the best leaders you've encountered. What made them exceptional? Often, it boils down to their genuine care for people and their intentionality. Effective leadership in children's ministry extends beyond merely delivering information or supervising activities. Your calling is to embody the heart of a shepherd, patiently guiding and nurturing the children entrusted to your care.

Think of it this way: Imagine you're a shepherd responsible for a flock of sheep. You wouldn't just herd them from one pasture to another; you'd pay attention to each one, ensuring they're healthy, fed, safe, and cared for. Similarly, as a children's ministry volunteer, you are called to shepherd the hearts of children, fostering an environment where they feel seen, valued, and genuinely loved. This transforms the ministry from a program-driven endeavor to a people-centered one, creating space for authentic relationships to blossom.

While you are not likely a trained therapist, your role is still to provide a compassionate presence, offer support, and connect children and families with appropriate resources when needed. Communicate with your ministry leader and together you can make a difference.

By going beyond the surface and recognizing the complexities of children's lives, children's ministries can foster a deeper sense of belonging, create a more inclusive environment, and ultimately, help children develop a stronger foundation of faith!

Partners,
Not Just Volunteers

Children's ministry thrives when fueled by a dedicated team. You are a vital part of the KidMin team! In fact, volunteers are the lifeblood of the ministry. You are more than someone who lends a hand; you are a partner in ministry, crucial to the success of KidMin. As partners, your contributions are essential in creating a thriving environment where children can grow in their faith.

Remember, the children's ministry doesn't rise and fall on any one person.

KidMin is about connecting with children, their families, and other volunteers on a personal and spiritual level. The goal is to partner with parents to guide children to Jesus and this goal is best accomplished together.

A Few Reminders as Partners, Not Just Volunteers:

Jesus valued kid's ministry. "But Jesus said, 'Let the children come to me. Don't stop them! For the Kingdom of Heaven belongs to those who are like these children'" (Matthew 19:14).

What you do matters, and your dedication does not go unnoticed. "For God is not unjust. He will not forget how hard you have worked for him and how you have shown your love to him by caring for other believers, as you still do" (Hebrews 6:10).

You are a valuable part of the team. "The human body has many parts, but the many parts make up one whole body. So it is with the body of Christ...But our bodies have many parts, and God has put each part just where he wants it... All of you together are Christ's body, and each of you is a part of it" (1 Corinthians 12:12, 18, 27).

Your unique gifts and talents allow you to connect with the children in a way no one else can. "Just as our bodies have many parts and each part has a special function, so it is with Christ's body. We are many parts of one body, and we all belong to each other. In his grace, God has given us different gifts for doing certain things well. So if God has given you the ability to prophesy, speak out with as much faith as God has given you" (Romans 12:4-6).

The next time the enemy leads you to believe, "I'm just a volunteer" come back to these scriptures and remind yourself how God has equipped you for this good work of kids ministry.

Thank you for your partnership in ministry! For real, thank you! You choose each week to show up and make ministry to kids possible. You choose to steward your gifts to build God's church. While so many people choose to sit on the bench, you are in the game giving it your all. Well done, good and faithful servant!

practical tools for
IMPACTFUL
ministry

When you're on an airplane, the flight attendant tells you to put on your own oxygen mask before assisting others. This rule is crucial because if you don't secure your own oxygen first, you might not be able to help anyone else. The same principle applies to serving in children's ministry: you need to take care of your own spiritual and emotional well-being first so you can effectively support and guide the children in your care.

It is vitally important to prioritize your own spiritual disciplines, like prayer and immersing yourself in Scripture. Proverbs 4:23 reminds us, "Guard your heart above all else, for it determines the course of your life." When facing challenges or seeking guidance, approach prayer with a posture of humble dependence on the Holy Spirit. Recognize the Holy Spirit is your constant companion, equipping and empowering you for the tasks of ministry.

Regularly examine your own walk with Christ. Are you growing in your faith? Are you allowing God's Word to transform your heart and mind? Seeking opportunities for personal spiritual growth will not only strengthen your own relationship with Christ but also equip you to better serve and guide the children in your care.

Remember, even superheroes need a little help sometimes! Don't be afraid to ask your leaders for help and for prayer. You are an important part of the team and the church needs you spiritually equipped for the long haul!

Preparation is Key

Effective children's ministry requires more than just showing up on Sunday. It demands a heart of dedication and intentional preparation that begins at the start of the week. This preparation involves not only logistical planning but also a deep consideration of the children's spiritual and emotional needs, all while seeking guidance and wisdom through prayer.

Prayer should be the cornerstone of preparation, starting as early as Sunday afternoon or Monday morning. This time set aside allows leaders to seek the

Holy Spirit's guidance in understanding the upcoming lesson and tailoring it to resonate with the children's lives. This proactive approach ensures the teaching is not merely information delivery, but a Spirit-led encounter with God's word.

Preparation extends to understanding the developmental phases of children. For instance, while preschoolers thrive in an environment where they are embraced, most preteens would rather have your affirmation. Tailoring teaching methods, activities, and even communication styles to these different stages creates a more impactful and engaging experience for everyone involved.

By welcoming prayerful preparation, which acknowledges the spiritual and emotional landscape of each child, leaders can create a children's ministry that extends beyond the walls of the church and into the everyday lives of the children they serve.

Hands-On Engagement

Children are not passive vessels waiting to be filled with information; they are active learners who thrive in engaging and interactive environments. Simply talking at children, even about the most important truths, often leads to disengagement. This is especially true with preteens. We need to be incorporating interactive activities, variety, and intentional involvement as key strategies to keep kids engaged.

As Deuteronomy 6:6-7 instructs, "And you must commit yourselves wholeheartedly to these commands that I am giving you today. Repeat them again and again to your children. Talk about them when you are at home and when you are on the road, when you are going to bed and when you are getting up."

Hands-on activities serve as a catalyst for making lessons stick. Instead of relying solely on lectures or traditional teaching methods, we need to engage children's senses and encourage active participation. Whether it's building a model of Noah's Ark with blocks, role-playing a Bible story, or participating in a game, hands-on experiences help children internalize concepts, fostering deeper understanding and retention.

Variety is essential to maintaining interest and addressing different learning styles. Be careful to not fall into the trap of a predictable routine. Just as children need a balanced diet for physical growth, they also need a balanced diet of teaching methods to stimulate their minds and spirits. Incorporating games, skits, object lessons, technology, outdoor activities, and even guest speakers can inject freshness and excitement into every lesson, catering to a wider range of learning preferences.

For example, what if the next time you were teaching about the walls of Jericho falling down, you had the kids march outside during part of the lesson? And what if you hung a red rope somewhere for the kids to discover themselves as they were marching? This hands on learning approach would stick in their minds and hearts far more than simply reading from a manuscript.

Inviting children to contribute their ideas, ask questions, and even lead certain aspects of the lesson transforms them from passive recipients to active participants. Consider also asking open-ended questions, facilitating group discussions, and creating opportunities for children to share their perspectives and experiences. This approach not only fosters a sense of belonging and importance but also encourages critical thinking and a deeper connection to the lesson.

The next time you are preparing a lesson, simply change your thinking to "show" rather than "tell" and you will be starting down the right path!

Creating an engaging and interactive learning environment requires intentionality, creativity, and a willingness to step outside of traditional teaching methods. By incorporating hands-on activities, embracing variety, and fostering intentional involvement, children's ministry leaders can create an environment where children are excited to learn, grow in their faith, and develop a lifelong love for God and His Word.

Preventative Discipline

In children's ministry, the goal is not simply to control behavior but to cultivate an environment where children feel safe, respected, and empowered to make positive choices. Reactive discipline addresses misbehavior after it occurs. Preventative discipline seeks to minimize those occurrences by proactively establishing clear expectations, nurturing positive relationships, and creating an engaging atmosphere that reduces the likelihood of disruptions.

A clearly defined plan and structure provides a framework for children to understand expectations and bound-aries. Be sure to establish clear rules, routines, and consequences that are communicated effectively and consis-tently enforced. This consistency helps children feel secure and understand the parameters of acceptable behavior.

Engaging and well-planned activ-ities are crucial for maintaining interest and preventing boredom, which can often lead to disruptive behavior. It's been said, "Make a plan, or the kids will make one for you!" If you are currently facing disciplinary issues, consider what role your leadership may play and make a plan to make next week's service better.

Preventative discipline is not a one-size-fits-all approach. It is an ongoing process requiring observation, adap-tation, and a genuine desire to create a positive and respectful learning environment for every child. By intentionally implementing these strategies, you can create a space where children feel loved, valued, and empowered to grow in their faith.

Empowering Parents

Parents are the primary spiritual influences in their children's lives. While you may have a few hours of influence in a child's life each week, parents have 10x hours of influence each day. While children's ministry volunteers are not meant to replace parents, they can provide significant support, encouragement, and resources to help parents navigate the joys and challenges of raising children in faith.

Connecting with parents on a personal level means building relationships beyond Sunday mornings to demonstrate genuine care and a stronger sense of community. This week you can make an effort to learn parents' names and to engage with them in conversation before or after services.

Consider offering practical support to families with young children, such as providing meals, running errands, or just asking if you can attend their next recital or game. Invite parents to participate in service projects or outreach opportunities alongside their children. Remember: Small gestures of kindness and support can make a significant difference in the lives of parents. By being intentional and proactive, you can help create a culture where parents feel empowered, equipped, and encouraged to raise their children in faith.

Communication is key. Regular communication helps parents feel connected and supported. You can make it a habit to share positive observations about their child's behavior or spiritual growth. Many parents only hear negative feedback and discipline issues. What if you began to find ways to brag about the kids and the growth you are seeing in their lives? Engage parents during pick-up and drop-off times with friendly conversation and relevant information about the day's lesson.

These small investments in the parents of the kids you are serving will pay dividends in the children's lives for decades to come!

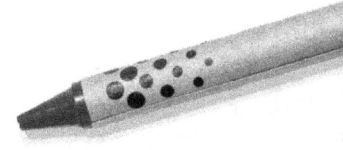

evaluating and
IMPROVING
ministry

No ministry can thrive without consistently evaluating and improving. Evaluating is more than just looking at numbers; it's about assessing the effectiveness of various aspects of the ministry to ensure it's leading children to Christ. This requires identifying areas that are successful and areas that need improvement.

Evaluating is the missing piece to most ministries, and it requires knowing the score and the rules of the game. It's important to be willing to ask tough questions in order to get an accurate assessment.

Just as in football, the team knows when they score a point and what it required to get there. You need to know what it's like to not only win but also what it's like to get a first down. 1 Corinthians 9:24-26a says, "Don't you realize that in a race everyone runs, but only one person gets the prize? So run to win! All athletes are disciplined in their training. They do it to win a prize that will fade away, but we do it for an eternal prize. So I run with purpose in every step."

The work God has called you to in kids ministry is vitally important and must be evaluated to ensure it is effective, fruitful, as well as aligned with God's mission and the vision of the church.

Setting Clear Goals

Rather than simply hoping for a large class or a successful Sunday experience, a thriving children's ministry must define what "winning" looks like by establishing SMART goals: goals that are Specific, Measurable, Achievable, Relevant, and Time-bound. These goals provide a road map for ministry, helping leaders focus their efforts and evaluate their effectiveness.

How To Apply the SMART Goal Framework

Specific: Goals should be clearly defined, leaving no room for ambiguity. Instead of a general goal like "improve our children's ministry," a specific goal might be setting a relational goal in a specific area like, "learning the names of every kid who walks through the door." This specific goal will push you in the direction of loving and leading the kids well.

Measurable: Establish concrete ways to track progress and determine if you've achieved your objective. If your goal is for kids to love coming to church, decide how you will measure success. Will you track the number of kids who return after their first visit, how many kids participate in the game you introduce, or will you decide to measure how many of your kids invite a friend? Keep in mind, it is also essential to ensure numeric goals don't overshadow the true mission of making disciples. Numbers matter, but remember it's not always about the numbers.

Achievable: Set realistic and attainable goals. Consider your resources, time constraints, and the specific context of your ministry. Setting overly ambitious goals can lead to discouragement and frustration, while setting easily achievable goals might not challenge you to grow. For instance, aiming for a small but significant improvement, like incorporating a new teaching element (such as scripture memorization) within a specific timeframe (two months), can be a more manageable and encouraging approach

Relevant: Goals should align with the overall mission and vision of both your children's ministry and your church. If your church emphasizes discipleship, outreach, or community engagement, your children's ministry goals should reflect those values. Regularly reviewing and adjusting goals as needed is important to ensure they remain relevant to the vision and direction of the church in this season.

Time-bound: Establish a clear timeframe for achieving your objectives. This creates a sense of urgency and allows for better tracking of progress. A time-bound goal might be "increase scripture memory participation by 15% by the end of the year" or "implement a new approach for how you intentionally welcome the kids to church within the next six months."

Setting SMART goals helps create a culture of intentionality and accountability within the ministry. Regularly review and evaluate your progress, celebrate victories, and make adjustments as needed to ensure you are effectively fulfilling your mission to reach and disciple the next generation.

Paul says it like this in Philippians 3:13-14, "No, dear brothers and sisters, I have not achieved it, but I focus on this one thing: Forgetting the past and looking forward to what lies ahead, I press on to reach the end of the race and receive the heavenly prize for which God, through Christ Jesus, is calling us."

Regular Feedback

Regularly gathering feedback from children, parents, and your ministry leader helps you gain valuable insights, identify areas for improvement, and foster a culture of transparency and collaboration.

Establishing a System for Regular Feedback

Children: While their feedback might be less structured, it's essential to create opportunities for children to share their thoughts and feelings about the ministry. This can be done informally through conversations or more formally through simple surveys with pictures, or designated feedback times during activities.

Asking age-appropriate questions like "What did you enjoy the most?" or "What would you like to learn more about?" can be valuable. Remember to prioritize making children feel heard and valued, even if their suggestions are not immediately implementable.

Parents: Parents are crucial stakeholders in the ministry, and their feedback can offer invaluable insights into their own perspectives on the ministry's effectiveness as well as their children's experiences. Make an effort to engage in casual conversations with parents during pick-up and drop-off times or at church events. These informal inter-actions can provide insights into parent needs and perspectives. Also consider attending parenting events put on by the church, even if you don't personally have kids. At these events you can learn more about what parents are experiencing and you can use the opportunity to encourage and connect with the parents of the kids in your ministry.

Ministry Leaders: Regular check-ins with your ministry leader ensures you are moving in an aligned direction with the whole kids ministry. Be brave and ask your ministry leader for specific feedback. Ask where they see you at your best and ask for a couple of areas where you can improve. Acknowledge this can be difficult to hear but that you are trying to grow in your ministry to kids.

When gathering feedback, prioritize creating a safe and non-judgmental environment where individuals feel comfortable sharing their honest opinions and experiences. Listen actively, ask clarifying questions, and express gratitude for their willingness to help improve. Remember, the ultimate goal of gathering feedback is to cultivate a culture of continuous improvement and create a children's ministry that effectively serves the needs of children, families, and volunteers alike.

Celebrating Successes

At your church, God is at work in the kid's ministry. He is worthy of recognition and we must actively look for ways to give Him credit for the work He is doing.

Acknowledge God's Sovereignty: Rather than attributing achievements solely to human effort, we need to shift the focus to God's provision and guidance. For example, when a new partner joins your ministry, acknowledge how the Lord is building the team and give Him credit for all the work He did to bring this volunteer to a place where they want to serve in kids ministry.

Practice Gratitude: Expressing gratitude keeps your heart from bitterness or entitlement. Stop right now and thank God for what He has done. Actually pray and express this gratitude to God using your words. Celebrating successes should be an act of worship, acknowledging God's faithfulness and provision.

1 Thessalonians 5:16-18 reminds our hearts to, "Always be joyful. Never stop praying. Be thankful in all circumstances, for this is God's will for you who belong to Christ Jesus."

Share Testimonies and Stories: There is so much power in sharing personal stories and testimonies of life change. Look for the stories and share them every chance you get. Psalms 66:16 says, "Come and listen, all you who fear God, and I will tell you what he did for me." Testimonies breathe life into ministry, revealing the tangible impact of God's work in the lives of individuals. Stories offer a powerful way to connect with others, inspire hope, and demonstrate the transformative power of faith.

Recognize the Value of Every Contribution: It's not just the efforts of one person who leads a child to faith. Everyone serving in the kids ministry has played a role in this salvation story. 1 Corinthians 3:6 says, "I planted the seed in your hearts, and Apollos watered it, but it was God who made it grow." Find ways to recognize everyone's work and help everyone celebrate, even those who serve behind the scenes.

Adaptive Strategies

The world shifts and changes every year, but what about your kids ministry? Rapidly changing culture requires ministries to embrace adaptability and innovation to remain effective and relevant, especially when ministering to the next generation. Clinging to outdated methods can lead to stagnation and disconnect, while a willingness to adapt and try new approaches can breathe fresh life into ministry.

There was a time in recent history where kids just showed up at church without any care about their safety.

Thankfully, those who went before us were willing to try new things and invest in technology and systems to make improvements that are standard in most churches today. Maybe God has placed something in your heart that will improve your kids ministry tomorrow or even kids ministry across the world for years to come! Isaiah 43:19 a says, "For I am about to do something new. See, I have already begun! Do you not see it?"

How to Cultivate Adaptability

Don't Fear Change: Many individuals and organizations resist change out of fear of failure or a desire for comfort and familiarity. However, refusing to adapt ultimately leads to decline. Just as in the natural world, growth often requires embracing new seasons and change. Kid's ministry leaders should encourage a spirit of flexibility and willingness to try new things, celebrating experimentation and viewing setbacks as opportunities for growth.

Constant Assessment: Regularly assess what's working and what's not in the ministry. Avoid simply replicating programs or approaches because "this is how it's always been done." Instead, be willing to ask tough questions, solicit feedback, and be open to making adjustments based on what you learn. This could involve tweaking existing programs, introducing new initiatives, or killing off a few sacred cows.

Tap into Creative Problem Solving: Encourage creative thinking within your team by fostering a culture of innovation and brainstorming. Embrace a "re-mix" mentality, finding fresh ways to present timeless truths in ways which resonate with the current generation. James 1:5 reminds us, "If you need wisdom, ask our generous God, and he will give it to you. He will not rebuke you for asking." Seeking God's wisdom can inspire innovative solutions.

Leverage Technology Thoughtfully: The digital age presents both challenges and opportunities for ministry. Be careful to not become reliant on technology, but find ways to leverage digital tools effectively to reach new audiences and enhance ministry impact. Explore digital platforms and multimedia content to create engaging and relevant experiences for today's tech-savvy generation. 1 Corinthians 9:22b-23 says, "Yes, I try to find common ground with everyone, doing everything I can to save some. I do everything to spread the Good News and share in its blessings."

By cultivating a ministry culture that embraces adaptation, you are playing your part in navigating the ever-changing landscape with resilience and creativity, ensuring your ministry remains fresh, engaging, and effective in reaching people for Christ.

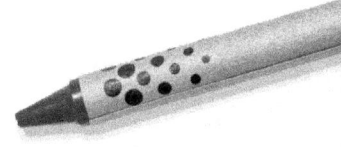

sustaining your
PASSION

Kid's ministry volunteer, you need to cultivate sustainable practices that prevent burnout and fuel long-term passion. This means prioritizing personal spiritual growth and soul care so ministry overflows from a heart filled with God's love and grace, rather than from empty reserves of human effort.

Ministry, even in its most joyful moments, demands significant time, energy, and emotional investment. You are susceptible to burnout when you neglect your own spiritual and emotional needs while pouring into the lives of others. This can lead to feelings of exhaustion and a diminished capacity to genuinely care. Recognizing the warning signs of burnout, such as feeling overwhelmed, apathetic, or resentful, is crucial for early intervention.

Just as a well must be replenished to continue providing water, so too must volunteers prioritize personal spiritual growth to effectively serve others.

How to Prioritize Personal Spiritual Growth

Be Intentional with Spiritual Practices: Scheduling dedicated time for prayer, scripture reading, and personal reflection is essential. These practices nourish the soul and help you connect with God's presence and guidance.

"Devote yourselves to prayer with an alert mind and a thankful heart."
-Colossians 4:2.

Seek Mentorship and Support: Connecting with other Christians, whether through mentorship, small groups, or trusted friends, provides a space for encouragement, accountability, and spiritual growth. Sharing struggles and triumphs within a supportive community fosters resilience and prevents isolation.

"As iron sharpens iron, so a friend sharpens a friend." -Proverbs 27:17

Embrace Rest and Sabbath: God's command to observe a Sabbath is not an optional suggestion, but a vital practice for spiritual, emotional, and physical well-being. Intentionally disconnecting from work and ministry responsibilities allows for rejuvenation and a renewed focus on God's presence.

"Then Jesus said, "Come to me, all of you who are weary and carry heavy burdens, and I will give you rest." -Matthew 11:28

Ministry as an Expression of Worship: Viewing ministry as an act of worship transforms mundane tasks into opportunities to honor and glorify God. This perspective shifts the focus from personal accomplishment to serving God wholeheartedly.

"Work willingly at whatever you do, as though you were working for the Lord rather than for people." -Colossians 3:23

Empower Others to Serve: Effective ministry involves equipping and empowering others to share in the work of serving. Delegating tasks, mentoring new volunteers, and fostering a culture of shared responsibility prevent burnout and multiply the impact of the ministry.

"You have heard me teach things that have been confirmed by many reliable witnesses. Now teach these truths to other trustworthy people who will be able to pass them on to others." -2 Timothy 2:2

Serving in kid's ministry is a high calling and a privilege. By prioritizing your own spiritual well-being, you can experience the joy and fulfillment of serving from a place of abundance, pouring into the lives of children and families for years to come.

Remember Your "Why"

Revisit your initial motivations for serving. Pause for a moment and remember when you first stepped into the role. Understanding the motivations behind our actions is crucial for long-term commitment, especially in kids ministry. When you can articulate your "why" for serving, you gain a clearer understanding of your role in fulfilling the larger mission of the ministry. This clarity fuels passion, strengthens resilience during challenging times, and fosters a deeper sense of purpose.

What initially drew you to serve? Was it a love for children, a desire to share your faith, a personal experience that ignited a passion for ministry, or a sense of calling from God?

What were your hopes and dreams when you first began? Did you envision impacting young lives, creating a welcoming community, nurturing spiritual growth, or being a positive influence?

Who were the people who inspired you along the way? Remembering the positive influence of mentors, pastors, or fellow volunteers can reignite a passion for serving.

How does your service contribute to fulfilling the mission? Think about concrete examples of how your individual roles, no matter how big or small they may seem, play a vital part in achieving the ministry's goals.

When you serve with a clear understanding of your "why," you become a powerful force for good in the kids ministry! Reconnect with your initial motivations to experience renewed passion, deeper purpose, and lasting joy in your service. If you rushed through those questions, I'd encourage you to go back and re-read this section to truly remember your "why!" Even if your only responsibility on Sunday morning is to pour goldfish crackers into small cups, you are playing a vital role in creating a welcoming and nurturing environment where children can encounter the love of Jesus. You are feeding the hungry. You are caring for the least of these. And I bet, you are playing a part in helping children feel loved and cared for within the church.

Build a Support Network

Children's ministry can be challenging, and having a network of people who understand these challenges can make a world of difference. Connecting with other children's ministry leaders provides a safe space to share experiences, both successes and struggles. Realizing that others face similar challenges can help combat feelings of isolation and provide valuable insights and advice.

A support network offers consistent encouragement and support, which are essential for navigating difficult seasons of ministry. Sharing burdens and celebrating victories together can help maintain a positive perspective and prevent burnout.

A network expands access to valuable resources, ideas, training opportunities, and practical advice for ministry challenges.

How to Build a Support Network

Connect with Other Kidmin Leaders: Invite other children's ministry leaders to lunch or coffee to foster relationships and establish connections.

Engage Online: Interact with online communities like the "I Love Kidmin" Facebook group to ask questions, find resources, and connect with other leaders.

Attend Conferences: Conferences aren't just for paid church staff. Attending a conference like KidzMatter helps you gain a fresh perspective, and gives training that equips you to better serve in your ministry context.

Seek Mentorship: Identify individuals within the church community with experience and wisdom in ministry, and seek their guidance.

Cultivate Relationships with Church Leadership: Foster open and honest communication with church leaders about the challenges, successes, and needs of the children's ministry.

Embrace Teamwork: Cultivate a culture of teamwork and collaboration within the children's ministry team. Ensure everyone on the team feels valued, heard, and empowered to contribute.

Lean into the Church: Collaborate with other ministries in the church to create a unified approach to discipleship and ministry and identify opportunities for shared resources and support.

Building a support network requires intentional effort and investment. By prioritizing connections with others, children's ministry leaders can cultivate a sense of belonging, receive much-needed encouragement, and access a wealth of resources that can sustain their passion for ministry.

Self-Care is Not Selfish

Serving from a place of depletion leads to burnout and negatively impacts both yourself and the ministry. When you prioritize your well-being, you can pour into the lives of children from a place of overflow and experience greater joy and longevity in your service.

Every day you face competing demands from work, family, and other commitments. Neglecting self-care can result in exhaustion and burnout, leading to decreased effectiveness and potential withdrawal from ministry.

Kid's ministry workers who prioritize their physical, emotional, and spiritual health can better embody the love and compassion of Christ. Self-care allows them to serve from a place of genuineness, not obligation.

When you prioritize self-care, you also model healthy boundaries and a balanced lifestyle for the children you serve. This sets a positive example for a lifestyle that values personal well-being alongside service.

Challenge the "Superhero" mentality in your teammates and yourself. View yourself as a valuable team member, not solely responsible for the ministry's success. Remember it's acceptable to have limitations and get help.

It's ok to take breaks. In fact, it's healthy and beneficial to take a break from serving, whether it's a week off, a season, or switching to a different role within the ministry. Taking a break reminds yourself the ministry doesn't solely rely on your shoulders.

To sustain your passion in children's ministry, prioritize your own well-being. Engage in spiritual practices, seek support, and embrace rest to avoid burnout. Reconnect with your initial motivations to keep your purpose clear and your passion strong. By taking care of yourself, you can serve from a place of abundance and make a lasting impact on the children you guide. Your role is vital and impactful—serve with joy, knowing your efforts contribute to an eternal legacy.

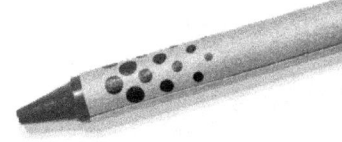

building a
LEGACY

A lasting legacy in children's ministry is about making a transformative impact on the lives of children that continues to shape their faith and values into adulthood. It's about raising up future leaders and equipping them to carry the torch of faith to the next generation.

You read this verse earlier in the book, but I want to remind you what Paul wrote to Timothy: "You have heard me teach things that have been confirmed by many reliable witnesses. Now teach these truths to other trustworthy people who will be able to pass them on to others" (2 Timothy 2:2).

Intentional Discipleship: Move beyond simply teaching children a lesson to fostering deep, personal relationships with Jesus. Guide children toward spiritual maturity and equip them to impact the world for Christ.

Empowering Future Leaders: Identify, equip, and empower emerging leaders within the ministry. Provide opportunities for them to discover and utilize their gifts, take on responsibilities, and develop their leadership capacity.

Cultivating a Culture of Reproduction: Create a ministry environment where discipleship and leadership development are ongoing cycles. Encourage and equip current leaders to mentor and train future generations, ensuring the ministry's values and vision continue.

Building a legacy is an ongoing process requiring intentionality, investment, and a willingness to adapt. By focusing on discipleship, leadership development, and a culture of reproduction, children's ministry can create a ripple effect that impacts generations to come.

Mentoring Future Leaders

Mentoring offers a unique space for experienced KidMin volunteers to impart wisdom, share practical skills, and nurture the spiritual growth of emerging leaders. This transfer of knowledge and experience is essential for maintaining continuity and fostering a thriving ministry. You may not be the most experienced or trained KidMin leader but I guarantee God has placed something inside of you worth sharing.

Investing in future leaders is not an additional task but a core value to the ministry's long-term success. There was a day when someone took the time to mentor and invest in you, now you need to share your experiences and all the Lord has taught you about kids ministry.

Establishing a clear framework for a mentoring relationship will start you off on the right foot. Outline a few goals, the frequency of meetings, and areas of focus. Think about some realistic expectations and what you hope the outcomes will be in your investment in the next generation of leaders.

Engaging in mentoring benefits the individuals you are pouring into as well as creates a ripple effect throughout the entire KidMin ministry. By cultivating a culture of mentorship, the ministry ensures a pipeline of leadership where the next generation of equipped and passionate leaders are prepared to step in.

As you mentor future leaders, the ministry's capacity for reaching and discipling children grows exponentially. By investing in mentoring, you create a lasting legacy of leadership development, ensuring that the vital work of impacting young lives continues for generations to come.

Creating Lasting Memories

Have you ever stopped to consider the work you do each week might end up in someone's personal testimony when they share their faith? Thoughtfully designed KidMin experiences can become woven into a child's faith story. These experiences transcend simple entertainment; they provide a foundation for spiritual formation and a deeper connection with God.

Creating Moments that Matter: Shift the focus from merely filling time to crafting experiences that resonate with a child's natural curiosity and desire for connection. Incorporate activities that foster wonder, encourage questions, and invite children to actively participate in their faith journey.

Integrating Sensory Experiences: Children, particularly younger ones, learn and connect through their senses. Incorporate elements into KidMin experiences that engage sight, sound, touch, and even smell. Consider incorporating visuals, music, hands-on activities, and even themed snacks to create a more immersive and memorable experience.

Leveraging the Power of Story: Stories have an unparalleled ability to capture a child's imagination and convey profound truths in relatable ways. Utilize storytelling in KidMin, incorporating interactive elements, costumes, and opportunities for children to participate in retelling biblical narratives.

The goal is to create a bridge between the lessons taught in KidMin and the memories children carry with them. When children are actively engaged, emotionally connected, and personally invested, the experience transcends passive participation and becomes a significant marker on their faith journey.

Solidify Biblical Truths: Engaging experiences transform abstract concepts into concrete memories, making biblical teachings more tangible and personally relevant for children. Through object lessons, these biblical truths can return to the child's memory outside of the church walls when they see the object you used in the teaching.

Cultivate a Love for Church: Positive and memorable KidMin experiences shape a child's perception of church, fostering a sense of belonging, excitement, and anticipation for participating in a faith community.

Plant Seeds of Faith: Engaging experiences create fertile ground for spiritual growth. Even if a child doesn't fully grasp the theological implications of an experience, the seed of faith is planted and can be nurtured over time.

Creating lasting memories requires intentionality, creativity, and a deep understanding of how children learn and connect. By investing in experiences that engage the heart, mind, and senses, your church can profoundly impact the spiritual journeys of children. You can play a part in creating a foundation of faith that shapes their lives for years to come.

Leaving a Spiritual Legacy

The last words of Jesus recorded in the book of Matthew say, "Therefore, go and make disciples of all the nations, baptizing them in the name of the Father and the Son and the Holy Spirit" (Matthew 28:19).

Your commitment extends far beyond the immediate impact on the children you serve. You are influencing future generations within the church as well as the broader community. The children you are discipling today will go on to continue building God's Kingdom for future generations. Your consistent presence, genuine care, and intentional discipleship create a ripple effect extending far beyond a single Sunday morning.

Children are incredibly perceptive, often learning more from what they observe than what they are explicitly taught. Kid's ministry leaders who consistently model a life of faith—through their actions, words, and attitudes—provide an invaluable example for children to emulate. This consistent witness to the transformative power of faith can leave a lasting impression on young hearts, shaping their understanding of what it means to follow Jesus.

By investing in young people, you contribute to the future leadership and spiritual vitality of the whole congregation. As young people experience the love and support of caring adults, they are more likely to remain connected to the church, eventually stepping into roles of service and leadership themselves. This repetitive pattern of discipleship helps ensure the continuation of a vibrant faith community for many years ahead.

Ultimately, the spiritual legacy fostered by dedicated volunteers is one of love and service. By pouring into the lives of children, you demonstrate the transformative power of Christ's love and inspire a new generation to live out their faith in tangible ways. This ripple effect of love and service has the potential to create lasting change within the church, community, and world.

Celebrating Milestones

Just as in any area of life, clear objectives provide direction and purpose. In children's ministry, milestones serve as markers of progress, helping everyone track their effectiveness and celebrate achievements along the way.

There is power in celebrating small wins. While it's natural to focus on significant events, the impact of celebrating smaller victories is catalytic. Recognizing consistent effort, personal growth, or steps in spiritual development can significantly boost morale and fuel ongoing commitment. Celebrate the ways

God moves in the ministry. Recognize answered prayers, changed lives, and spiritual growth, shifting the focus from human effort to divine influence.

This call to serve in the kid's ministry is a marathon. Don't just celebrate the end of the race when you hear God say, "Well done, good and faithful servant." Celebrate all along the way. Celebrate when a child takes the initiative to lead a prayer. Celebrate when a child memorizes and recites a Bible verse they have forever hidden in their heart. Celebrate when a child takes the step of being baptized and publicly declares their faith. Celebrate when a child shows compassion or kindness, reflecting on the Bible lesson they just learned.

Take a moment, right now, to reflect on God's faithfulness by asking yourself,

"When was the last time I witnessed a child take a step forward in their walk with the Lord?" As 1 Thessalonians 5:18 advises, "Be thankful in all circumstances, for this is God's will for you who belong to Christ Jesus."

And speaking of celebrating milestones, congratulations on reaching the end of this book. I really am proud of you for investing your time and energy into the ministry where God has called you to serve. Now before you go on to the next thing on your to-do list, take a moment to thumb back through the book and see if there is anything God wants you to focus on right now. Ask the Holy Spirit to guide you and then write down your next step.

My Next Step: _____

_____

_____

_____

_____

_____

_____

_____

_____

_____

_____

_____

_____

_____

_____

_____

_____

_____

_____

A Prayer For You

Heavenly Father, thank You for those who have gone before us and those who will come after us committing their time and energy to serving in children's ministry. Bless us with wisdom, patience, and joy as we guide young hearts towards You. May we always feel Your presence and find strength and encouragement in Your Word. Let our efforts bear eternal fruit, and may we please you with our service. In Jesus' name, Amen.

About Corey Jones

Corey has served as a Kids Pastor and Next Gen Pastor from 2006 to 2020. He currently serves as the Executive Pastor at Southern Hills in Georgia and strives to be an opportunist, learner, and helper. His mission is to help leaders take their next step in personal development. Find out more at CoreyRayJones.com

www.ingramcontent.com/pod-product-compliance
Lightning Source LLC
Chambersburg PA
CBHW070724130626
46553CB00005B/2137